Sanctuaries

By the same author

Sanctuaries

Diane Fahey

PUNCHER & WATTMANN

First published in 2024
Published by Puncher & Wattmann
PO Box 279
Waratah NSW 2298

info@puncherandwattmann.com

NATIONAL
LIBRARY
OF AUSTRALIA

A catalogue record for this book is available from The National Library of Australia.

ISBN   9781923099289

Cover photograph: *Taking in the Vista* by Stefan Christmann (detail)
        https://nature-in-focus.de
Cover design by David Musgrave
Printed by Lightning Source International

Contents

Company Terms

A Summoning of Birds

Proem

Birdscapes

Ways of Being

The Moments

2. *Sightings*

Foreword by Gisela Kaplan

To have been asked to write a foreword to this book of poetry on birds – its contents exciting, analytical, aesthetically pleasing and contemplative – is a real honour. As a scientist and specialist on bird biology and behaviour I can say that Diane Fahey is ever so insightful and always correct in even the smallest glimpses of biological or behavioural aspects of a species that she observes.

We probably all read far too little poetry. It is a genre that is irreplaceable because of its rich and surprising intimations of matters of deep relevance, and because it makes us feel, think and perceive in new ways – in this collection of poems, even training our inner gaze on a bird in the wild not otherwise given a second thought by us.

Diane Fahey is already a distinguished poet, and it shows in her craft and the succinctness of her style. Her poetry made me laugh, re-read lines, or even almost cry because of finding it so beautiful. How beautiful and unexpected is the following:

Mute swans

form pictograms from
unknown languages, write with
mango beaks on lakes,
move at will from one kind of
perfection to another.

Diane Fahey is also very contemporary, not shying away from making scant but powerful references to what we do to living species, and to the ever-dwindling forests of Australia.

First and foremost, *Sanctuaries* is a book that one can read leisurely, savouring each poem like a good glass of wine, making one appreciate what was not seen before. The poet's sharp photographer's eye captures many elusive and memorable details – a bird's plumage, sometimes barely noticed, becoming a kaleidoscope of brilliant colours – all made present through words.

There is nothing obscure in her poetry – it's like a brightly lit art gallery where one can stop and feast on each image, invited in. I hope that many will take up the invitation and partake of the unique pleasures of this book and the highlights of celebrating birds generally and native Australian birds specifically.

The title *Sanctuaries* is very apt – it is not just a reference to the separate lives of birds but to the sanctuary we might find in the natural world and be happier for doing so, if we just dare.

Gisela Kaplan, AM

prof. em. in Animal Behaviour, UNE, Science and Technology, Armidale, NSW, 2351
Book Author of *Australian Magpie, Tawny Frogmouth, Bird Minds, Bird Bonds* and others.

The Mirrors

The Mirrors

I

Backstory

Presumed male,
though that may be a fiction:
the matter never resolved.

Origin, somewhere in Africa.
Brought here from Hamburg
in 1933.

Of advanced age, therefore,
in 2008
when set upon by youths

who would be apprehended,
detained, let go –
no witnesses, case dismissed –

one of them giving the finger
to reporters outside the Court.
The lads, one a ward of the state,

all from 'the outlying districts',
then sped off through the streets –
nothing to see here,

their victim, after all,
ticked so many boxes,
almost, you might say, asking for it:

frail, with a foreign otherness,
strange-coloured, voiceless,
and having nowhere to hide.

But – bashed, wounded in one eye –
he fought to come back,
the surgeon had said,

so that he won a stay of life,
dying in 2014
after more brave years

with the solace of being
much loved, much visited,
and companioned by Chile,

presumed female,
his partner in loneliness
for four decades.

His name was Greater –
after Alexander the Great, some thought,
the truth less grandiose.

Home

This photo from 1920
shows where they lived:

the flamingo enclosure
at the Adelaide Zoo.

In a sunlit pond
shadowed by tall trees,

a group of twelve –
the elegant riddle of

their hook-like necks,
hump-like bodies, stilt legs

cast darkly afloat upon
that sepia shimmer,

almost undone by it.
Some may have survived

beyond the advent of Greater,
the Greater Flamingo,

none, by the time of Chile,
the Chilean Flamingo:

Greater, living long enough
to become, it was believed,

the oldest flamingo
in the world,

Chile outliving him until,
far gone with arthritis,

she was euthanised
in 2018.

It was determined, then,
that she was indeed female:

the last flamingo
to live in Australia –

our final fling of flamingos:
none may be brought here now.

Portraits

I've printed out photos
of Greater, of Chile,

each more intricately composed
than a studio portrait –

flamingos being unable to escape
the condition of art –

always exquisite, with their famed
chrysanthemum plumage,

yet always creaturely,
beguilingly aware,

those planetary eyes,
each with a tiny black moon,

expressing the patient mystery
of their presence in life.

Mirror

There are articles, too –
one tells me that a keeper,

after Greater's death,
installed a mirror

in the Flamingo Grotto,
now Chile's domain

where – duskily filmed
or with a watery dazzle –

a flamingo kept her company,
a silent ghost

with her own eyes
shining back at her.

Word has it she took
no notice of the mirror.

Word has it she missed
Greater until her death.

How could she not?

II

Timeline

1

During their heyday there were more species of flamingo
living in Australia than anywhere else in the world –
up to as many as five species at one time.
– Dr Adam Yates

For twenty million years, or so,
until one million years ago,
or so, flamingos inhabited
the wetlands and shallow lakes
that covered central Australia –
all six species of them,
the greater flamingo
the last to go.

Their algae-fed bones,
so durable, lie far beneath
that heartland of, now,
red desert, ochre moonscapes
and – in the rare years
of measureless rain –
an inland sea
miraculously hosting waterbirds
amidst desert greenness.

2

Euelpides: *By Zeus, that's a bird? What kind would you call that?*
 It couldn't be a peacock, could it? …
Tereus: *Not your everyday fowl – the kind you always see.*
 She's a marsh bird.
Euelpides: *My goodness, she's gorgeous – flaming red!*
Tereus: *Naturally, that's why she's called Flamingo.*
– Aristophanes' *The Birds*

In ancient Egypt
the flamingo hieroglyph
meant 'red' – the redness
which had given them the name
phoenicoptere,
linked them with the flaming phoenix.

For emperors of the madder kind
in Roman times,
some were caged and fattened at Baiae –
their pickled tongues served on platters.

The poet Martial pondered
a different fate for flamingos,
could they sing.

Caligula, who sacrificed them to the gods,
was sprayed with flamingo blood,
by accident, on the day of his assassination.

3

*… although I saw a great number of them in the course of my stay
in that country, I cannot even at this moment boast of having had
the satisfaction of shooting a single individual.*
– John James Audubon, on the flamingos of Key West

Explorers from Europe –
first sightings logged then capture or slaughter –
would take back sketches, narratives of pursuit,
specimens alive or dead.

In due course, in the Americas,
flamingos would be mapped out
by nature artists –
Audubon taking their graceful
singularity to its limit:
his American flamingo
shown with ruby-red neck
in eerie parallel to
the line of a leg,
its ever-unfolding image
momently fixed
in gothic submission.

In later years, sport hunting,
plume hunting – the art of the hat
wantonly embellished.

Later still, flamingos
became creatures of fantasy, whimsy.
On a croquet lawn, Tenniel's Alice
holds one, an honorary mallet
tucked under an arm,
her right foot pressed down
on a hedgehog:

the bird and the child
in unchosen closeness,
eye to coldly affrighted eye.

Our imaginations, it would seem,
will seize on anything
as we revel in the exotic,
raising tinctured potions to our lips
at the cocktail hour
in some cruiseship-sleek, retro venue
called *The Flamingo Bar* –
along its walls, a frieze evoking
the steaming swamps of, say,
Florida,
so far away, so near.

Meanwhile, antithetically,
flamingos have colonised the U.S.,
marooned on countless suburban lawns
in mauve plastic. Inviolable.

Let the rains come
until rivulets form, releasing
metal legs from hard-packed earth,
let it keep on raining until
a deluge lifts, sweeps away
all those cryptic guardians
and floats them down to Florida:

eidolons swaying amongst the real
in the twilight of the everglades
as unearthly glints slide across
ersatz wings, across
true, growing feather.

4

Despite being the most numerous species of flamingo,
[the lesser flamingo] is classified as near threatened due to
its declining population and the low number of breeding sites,
some of which are threatened by human activities.
– Mark D. Anderson

Lake Natron, now:
its mudflats still, though precariously,
their largest breeding site in the world.

Across a sky-veiled mirror –
into which small birds on epic journeys
have been known to crash –

flocks of lesser flamingos feed
from alkaline water:
aerial photographs give us

archipelagos the colour of plum blossom,
mosaicked glyphs slowly transforming –
fractal flamingos.

               *

In Tanzania, now,
industrialists and others
would like to make, shall we say,

inroads, so as to access
Lake Natron and its resources,
build a soda ash plant on its shores.

If so, as at Kenya's Lake Magadi,
the water level will drop,
the pH levels change

and the flamingos,
those connoisseurs of toxicity,
will begin to leave –

quietly, company by company,
with only the drama of their black-bordered wings
as they ascend into sacred blue.

Continuance

1

At San Diego Zoo, a resident flamingo flock
stopped breeding for 14 years, after several
of their flock-mates were relocated. After new
birds were brought in, breeding continued.

To fire up
hormone production,
flamingos engage in
'head-flagging', 'wing salute'
and marching (with abrupt turns).

But in truth
some conditions for mating
are beyond subtle,
with, for instance, flock numbers
of key importance.

And in captivity,
attempts at mating
may fail, should the male
find no sure grip
on her clipped wings.

2

Some facilities have attempted to trick the birds into
thinking they have more neighbours by installing
mirrors throughout their flamingo enclosures…
– Caitlin R. Kight

Mirrors, not as an *aide-mémoire*
but as a provocation
to mate,

mirrors as shining affirmations
of a collective that will
protect and buffer,

help shield new life –
survival of the one
linked to the survival of all

once the magic number
is reached, the flock's
critical mass.

3

… however, aviculturist Phil Tovey reports that this causes some
narcissistic birds to become a bit self-obsessed and spend more
time looking at their own reflections than wooing potential mates.
– Caitlin R. Kight

Who said that, of all the birds,
only magpies
can know themselves in mirrors?

But perhaps what we have here
is something we ourselves know about:
the other as an elusive mistake,

a taunting projection –
a companion who seems perfect,
is always there, sharing our gaze,

but who, coming towards us,
can never quite reach us
and vanishes when we draw close.

4

In the wild, flamingos
whether thriving or diminishing in number,

flock in multiples of multiples –
massed, wondrously as one,

each engaged in the great work
of survival, of furthering life

as, grounded in mud,
they circle themselves or meander,

filter-feeding through
the alchemical chambers of their beaks.

*

With their necks' ingenious reach
flamingos outswan the swan,

groom with ease
the furthest feathers,

rest small, beak-heavy heads
congenially, against a wing.

Elliptical bodies
ballast their lankiness –

a finely tuned accord between
the upright, the horizontal.

*

Compositely,
flamingos vie with

the lotus, the camellia,
in offering matchless shades

of pink, of red,
along with the sheerest white –

life colours, soul colours,
solace to the human eye.

5

On nests shaped from mud,
a single egg is tended until
    tap, tap, tap
a ragged portal appears.

The chick, feet and legs
a crinkled pinkness,
plumps out as its down dries
in the warm, wide air.

It will rest, later,
under the haven of a wing,
its straight grey beak
upraised to receive

from that baroque beak,
orange and black,
larger than the chick itself,
a liquid sourced from algae

and from the feeding parent's blood,
a red elixir falling
    drop by slow drop,
        the chick tonguing it in.

Coda

The Way of Things

Cruelty
travels with us,

it is always there,
abroad in our shared world

like a disembodied
black wing, metallically

bright, flapping above us,
slicing the sun in half.

And it can travel within us
like a second pulse:

a heavy quickening
in the blood-washed heart,

in the fraught, fragile brain –
seeding phantoms that promise

some terrible form of
comfort, of release:

a transference of pain and fear
from one life to another.

Encounter

If I could sit down
with those youths, men now,
(yes, this is a fantasy)

sit down, bringing as always
my flaws and faults,
my good intentions,

what might I say?
Or perhaps I would simply
wait on through the silence

until one of them
chose to speak,
or they all, as suddenly as

birds lift into flight,
got up and left?
I would wait on until

someone came to an empty chair
to look into my eyes,
to challenge me,

the both of us held there,
hoping for hope,
for some new imprinting.

Zoo Birds

Meditation

Icons of the art
of now, of being nowhere
but here, they practise
pure stillness, freedom from thought.
Then hunt a little. Herons.

Cormorant

Acts of housekeeping
really, so why this sense of
sacredness as wings
open like pages, angle
themselves to meet the wind's gaze.

Mute swans

form pictograms from
unknown languages, write with
mango beaks on lakes,
move at will from one kind of
perfection to another.

Mallards

with sequined green heads,
cobalt wing-panels, change to
feathery icebergs
as they feed from the depths, rise
with iridescent sang-froid.

Mandarin ducks

Enamelled by light
they enthrall, like wondrous toys.
Their waterproof gaze
deflects empathy, linkage,
stays blithely unreadable.

Mandarin ducks at the cascade

Not too beautiful
to enjoy life, they jump, twirl
over the maelstrom
in multiple uniqueness,
climb again to the stone ledge.

Glossy ibis

So eerily red –
a Mephistopheles bird.
Nest, built high in sedge.
Just a touch of Art Deco,
with Egyptian blue-green eggs.

Pied heron

A timeless silence.
Its gaze, memoried by seas,
wetlands, vast rivers,
enters, so it seems, my own.
The glass lake darkens, glimmers.

Rescued pelicans

In a white coven
they swim, keeping their counsel
amidst the honking,
the screeching – wise and weighty,
magnificently present.

Flamingos, Singapore

In khaki water,
mercifully in a flock,
they sift diatoms
or, like statues come to life,
raise pliant necks, powerhouse beaks.

A colony of cormorants

dwells in this idyll
of dead branches, phony rocks,
glassed-in, brackish pool –
plagued by chafed skin, flightlessness,
and, if they knew it, by time.

Hummingbird nest

Brought to Singapore
by long-dead sailors – cobwebbed
pouch once packed with throats
not yet ruby, breasts not yet
sapphire, wings never to whirr.

Golden pheasants

Nature invented art,
they remind us – gripped by
their need to seed self-
copies ad infinitum:
each one a mobile Venice.

Common pheasant

Plumage: chestnut-brown,
copper-red, slippery gold
sheened purple and green.
Hints of junglefowl, peafowl –
and a rumour of phoenix.

Lady Amherst's pheasants

True aristocrats.
Bodies, solid as trust funds;
each tail, a poised quip.
Head-capes, fanned wide in display,
show them artfully one-eyed.

In the parrot precinct

Patagonian
parrots wear landscape colours:
earth, clay, rock. Conures
celebrate high noon. The rest,
bright fruits, leaves, the bluest skies.

Macaws

A rainforest – *this*?
They congregate on dry boughs
under the glass dome:
bitter gossip, a cracking
silence like that of felled trees.

African greys

They snub pleasantries,
obsidian eyes agleam –
each glance shrewd, icy.
If revenge were to be had,
what torture would they devise?

Corella

She swoops in, close to
the heads of the audience,
does tricks as required,
talks back with quizzical zest.
Flirty eyes, bright as gumdrops.

Orange-bellied parrot

Such a shy presence
in this roofed domain of doves,
fairy wrens, firetails –
all safe, none of them free: each
an indelible story.

Superb pittas

Blackly radiant.
Wings of sky glitter, green-tipped.
Belly, cinnabar.
Called 'jewel thrushes'. Endangered.
Their home is Manus Island.

Wompoo fruit-doves

Blow-ins from the North
who've ventured down the east coast's
dwindling rainforests.
Picture-book bright, they beguile
in yellow, plum-purple, green.

Bleeding-heart pigeon

A crimson stab-wound
on its delta of sluiced red –
a living symbol
set off by plumped beige, flint grey:
the shades of *schadenfreude*.

Grey butcherbirds

Clever, cruel, they wear
an arcane look, dour in black,
grey, with clerical
collar. Their song? – brook water
burbling on stones, scalpel-sharp.

White-browed woodswallows

As if apprised of
their own beauty, they perch in
blessed stillness. Beaks,
pale blue; breasts – cinnamon, hers,
chestnut, his. A silvery muse.

Tawny frogmouths

Almost nose to beak
you can watch furred clumps, cute as
kittens, on a bough –
incognito dreamers, eyes
clamped against light, this cage, you.

Peacock

From a concrete ledge
that orgasmic cry – so harsh,
unlovely. The tail
cascades down, spying on poised
cameras, toddlers' tears, popcorn.

Satin bowerbird

Purple-black plumage
sleek, sexy, he sets the stage –
a twigged crucible
strewn with blue glitz. He's a star,
primed for the dance of his life.

Paired brolgas

Untranslatable
flows of feeling between them,
they saunter around
this crabbed space wherein they'll mate,
nest, charm each other with dance.

Greater bird-of-paradise

Once, on boughs near clouds,
acrobatic moves all day,
the flounce and flick of
plumes – yellow, airy silver;
many ticks on the dance card.

Azure-winged kookaburra

Voice: extended maniac laughter
– Field Guide

An old chuckler with
summer skies emblazoning
her wings; the browns of
wattle bark and river dirt:
an uncanny completeness.

Regent honeyeater

An intricate mesh,
black on gold, as when lights dim
in an opera house.
No diva, its mesmeric
faint call chimes from the chorus.

Superb lyrebird

In his ferny patch
he conjures them, pitch-perfect:
whipbird and bellbird,
lorikeets, black cockatoos,
the exiled crimson macaws.

Black-faced cuckoo-shrike

Eyes, brimming with light.
Its true habitat, alas,
is open woodland.
It speeds through a leafy maze,
back and forth, again, again.

Bird of prey centre

I find the cages –
empty, except for that prince
tethered to a stake.
A gaze that could encompass
mountains, wings that could cross them.

Rufous owl

In the night creatures enclosure

Her bright yellow eyes
become black moons when the lights,
on a time switch, dim.
Still clear: grey beak, the striped down's
unnecessary beauty.

Company Terms

Company Terms

*A list of nouns designating birds in groups
appears in* The Book of Saint Albans *of 1486.
These are called 'company terms'.*

a wind-map of gulls
a wounded sea of gannets
a quell of kingfishers
a regatta of swans
an Escher of geese
a snow globe of egrets
a sky-robe of starlings
a candlelit forest of owls
a bluebelled field of fairy wrens
a pinnacle of skylarks
a downpour of umbrella birds
an optimism of robins
an eisteddfod of blackbirds
a ventriloquy of lyrebirds
a seance of woodpeckers
a funeral wake of stone curlews
a sound barrier of falcons
a grand opera of hornbills
a tableau vivant of sicklebills
an immanence of manucodes
an efflorescence of riflebirds
a synergy of manakins
a levitation of grebes
a terpsichore of cranes
a croquet set of flamingos
a Versailles of peacocks
a Déjeuner sur l'herbe of galahs
a Gauguin of rainbow lorikeets
a Fabergé of goldfinches

a masked ball of bee-eaters
a piracy of ravens
a dungeon of butcher birds
a crime scene of condors
an identity parade of penguins
an interrogation of crested cockatoos
a judiciary of jackdaws
a jury of godwits
a legal team of eagle-owls
an advocacy of avocets
a courtroom of crossbills
an innocence of albatrosses
a census of sparrows
a consensuality of love birds
a loneliness of shoebills
a grand hotel of rock pigeons
a footnote of passenger pigeons
a dwindle of *cinclodes palliatus*
a limbo of kākāpō
a display case of dodo
a silence of nightingales

A Summoning of Birds

The Roosting Island

They've flown down through lemon light
to this shadowy hotchpotch of trees –

herons, cormorants, ibis
a community now, spread through tiers of branches.

Restive groups wheel over the lake, resettle.
Incoming dusk shrouds, first, the little black cormorants,

rickety lines of egrets start to glow.
Each bird, at each moment, complete, beautiful.

Waterways, Skyways

a water meadow of silver teals
a mandala'd pond of moorhens

a skid of pintails
a slow-motion take-off of loons

a lifted lake of snow geese
a storyline of greylag geese

a victory sign of mallards
a fluttering moon of black swans

Coast, Ocean

a storeyed cliff of puffins
an outcrop of shags

a shore-sweep of spoonbills
a mirage of sanderlings

a pelagic swell of razorbills
a polar wind of shearwaters

a lyric odyssey of tropicbirds
a flying island of terns

Afar

a nirvana of Himalayan eagles
a plumed canopy of birds-of-paradise

a savanna of secretary birds
a steppe of bustards

a Texan prairie of burrowing owls
a nest-heaped scrubland of Mallee fowl

a Kenyan lake, caustic and hot, of lesser flamingos
an Antarctic of skimmers, skuas, storm petrels, sheathbills

Among the Trees

a fig tree of fruit doves
an olive tree of turtle doves

a pear orchard of partridges
a globed arboretum of weaverbirds

a sculpture garden of satin bowerbirds
a butterfly bush, pink, of scarlet honeyeaters

a labyrinth of wattlebirds, pardalotes
a leaf-framed gallery of golden whistlers, blackbirds

Presences

a composure of herons
a surety of stilts

a busyness of coots
a playfulness of loons

a conviviality of waxwings
a confidingness of robins

an audacity of grackles
a prescience of griffons

Gatherings

a levee of sparrows on the dewed lawn
a fan club of willie wagtails

a colloquium of rooks
a lek of cocks-of-the-rock

doyen of group-breeders, the chestnut-crowned babbler –
nests with live-in helpers, communal dust-bathing, games

a caterpillar of twelve bee-eaters on a bough –
green visited by mauve, with sun-gold trim

In Motion

a nuptial sky-dance of bald eagles
a leaping of jewel-throated jabiru

a somersault of chickadees
a breakdance of white cockatoos

an edible geometry of swifts
a wheel of northern shovelers, rummaging

a flummox of quail
a Highland Fling of woodcocks

Pace

a velocity of ostriches
a dust devil of roadrunners

a cloud of blue-footed boobies raining down on a shoal
a company of black cockatoos, conversing as they fly

a runway of albatross chicks tipping the waves, learning lift-off
a plunging promenade of jacana chicks

a royal progress of swans, cygnets underwing
a summer holiday of ducklings

On the Attack

the mobbing of a red-tailed hawk by crows
the mobbing of a crow by mockingbirds

the arced stoop of a peregrine, surprise the key
the hush of a great horned owl guided towards a peregrine

a clash of helmeted hornbills, head to casqued head
a tourney of ruffs, *philomachus pugnax,* wearing lurid ghostheads

the ferocious rebuff of white-winged choughs, eyes engorged
the panache of hummers, seeking primacy among the blooms

Ascendancies

the shoebill, *balaeniceps rex,* 'king whalehead',
ingester of lungfish, baby crocodiles: status, 'vulnerable'

wearers of crowns: the hoopoe, the black crowned crane,
the blue crowned pigeon, the royal flycatcher

two crowns of anther-tipped filaments above lofty necks –
peahen and peacock equal, at least, in this

borne on an eagle's back, Aristotle's wren flies upward
as its host descends, wins the title 'King of the Birds'

Stratagems

a collusion of cormorants
a co-operative of fairy wrens

a toolkit of New Caledonian crows
a memory bank of nutcrackers

an El Dorado map of honeyguides
a nest invasion of cowbirds

hooded plovers, their staged surrenders
sky-sweeping nighthawks, at one with tree bark, woodland floor

The Great Round

survival by beauty – among songbirds
he wears the best colours but, mostly, she chooses

survival by care – mostly, she broods
but partnerships abound:

tag teams flitting to and fro
with twigs, wriggling sustenance

a new life unlocks itself: the helplessness, the triumph
grebe chicks in their chariots of down

Nests

a translucent curve, shaped from saliva by the white-nest swiftlet
chambered in a eucalypt hollow, the nest of the quarrion

more down-home, the mound or ground nest
the brave risk of a hooded plover's scrape

the coot's nest, weavings of leaves, stems, roots
among the lily pads

sky-platforms built by ospreys –
invincible splendour in a wild sea of air

Wherever, However

nests of peat, twigs, penguin feathers: the southern albatross
flat nests of stones culled by Adélie penguins

under Arctic winds, nests of the snow bunting –
between rocks, within crevices of rocks

nests of the white stork in Belozem, in Altreu,
a meta-architecture on town rooftops

a brown dipper's nest: domed, with side entrance,
a view of its second home

Eggs

a nest of four bluebird eggs, blue,
one cowbird egg, brown

a thimbleful of vervain hummingbird eggs, white
a floating nest of jacana eggs: black curlicues on mahogany

on a high ledge, the murre's tapered egg, its shell a map of islands
a life forestalled: that turquoise eye on the path

the shock of one egg found inside another
the broken cradling the complete

Eyes

the blink of a bee hummingbird
the flashing of a dipper's white eyelids, camouflage in tumbling water

the eye-cloak of a loggerhead shrike, milky blue
a cormorant's third eyelid, windowed for underwater viewing

within the catchlight of a wren's eye, a silhouette of trees
a circlet of quills rimming a robin's eye: reeds around a pool

on its nape, the eye patches, ever alert, of the pearl-spotted owlet
tears of the black-chinned antbird, siphoned as it sleeps by a moth

Translations

at Broome, mighty lift-offs of godwits, red knots, the eastern curlews
by the Yellow Sea, feeding grounds of red knots, eastern curlews, godwits

an Arctic tundra of summer guests: eastern curlews, red knots, godwits et al.
here, now, resting in burrows, shearwaters home from the Bering Sea

above the Gulf of Mexico, hosts in travail, sky-bedimming –
glints of ruby-throated hummingbirds

east-west flyways of geese and swans, of raptors
the gentle hordes of redwings, fieldfares, bramblings

Threat

a sky-tide of golden-winged warblers homing down into Appalachia,
surging up again, five days before the tornado

a sodality of geese, descended to a rest stop, lift suddenly upward
leaving, as they must, the one trapped in a dark spill

around the Mediterranean, ancient nets heavy with
almost weightless songbirds

the sport killing of, for instance, wood duck, mountain duck, chestnut teal
– deaths quick or slow, broods left unguarded

Murmurations

a billow of starlings at play with invisibility
each an image of Mozart's caged muse

a sky of shape-shifters, all of one mind,
of veils, masks, a magician's cape with silver lining

a shadow world of inverse mountains,
apocalyptic seas, sway-backed leviathans

in the space of a breath:
creation, uncreation, resurgence

Glimpse

winged bodies glide above Little Skellig, the great gannetry –
as the boat turns away, dolphins

risen from the horizon, a procession of pelicans
climbs past this mountain isle, each a different shape in the wind

robins, perhaps? – a birdscape travelling over the winter fields
lifting toward plumes of cirrus, lost in the sun

last gleam of a diamante necklace,
the sky, manucode-blue

Apparitions

the window-tapping of mudlarks, a folly of the mating season
on a pool of rain, a *doppelgänger* magpie, canny-eyed

first light reaches herons nested high in the forest –
calmly at home under dumpling clouds, the eye of a drone

a subliminal flicker of mountain bluebirds
a chartreuse ghost of canaries, finessing the desert air

on a balustrade, a white peacock, its cascading train
emblazoned by moonlight

Visible, Invisible

the scarlet-banded barbet of Peru,
newly discovered, rare, vivacious in the tree tops

the hidden gaze of the cloud forest pygmy-owl –
scourge of voles, grasshoppers, crickets

a zigzag of snipe, exquisitely fugitive among the tussocks
a ricochet of swallows

sky traffic of cormorants, black or pied, silver gulls, ibis –
wayward, purposive dances that end, as one blinks, in blank space

Camouflage

a *trompe l'oeil* of frogmouths
a swatch of rogue bark travelling upward: the tree creeper

an undulant mat barred with brown, stone-grey, black –
a ptarmigan hugs scree, dead bracken, the spring earth

nightjars, an uncanny match with gravelled roadsides, leaf fall –
harmless swipers of insects, feared harbingers of death

the face and breast of a snowy owl, at one with her albino world
wings, vertiginous; eyes, furnace-yellow

Patterns

under ripped clouds, rays of smoky light, smoky darkness:
a raptor, halving the sky, cuts through them

shadow-weave of kelp gulls, terns, pelicans over a sunlit bay:
you have entered a mind, eagle-high, gannet-deep

a convocation of ravens gather, crisscrossing in the bright air
I stand, striped by their shadows

archived in black and white: starlings lift from bare branches
– a vast new crown flutters its summer foliage

A Litany of Colour

lapis lazuli of the black-naped monarch
the yellow of a gannet's head: soul-lifting, soul-soothing

the magnetic presence of the lilac-breasted roller,
of the turaco with its purple crest, of the violet-green swallow

a kaleidoscope of macaws –
the hyacinth, the golden-collared, the scarlet

an accidental rainbow of Gouldian finches
a whole sky of blue jays

Studies in Red

eclectus parrots: his emerald points up her ruby-red –
head and breast deeply bright, a burgundy mantle, royal-blue trim

the vermilion flycatcher – crewcut and bodysuit, flame-red
every feather of the summer tanager, strawberry-red

the black mask of the northern cardinal –
burglar or carnival reveller? – all else, red, red, red

the red-capped robin, bearer of hope, comfort:
a red like no other

Splendour

an epiphany of peacocks
egrets in their bridal attire

an iridescence of hummingbirds –
the violet-tailed sylph, the red-tailed comet

the golden-headed quetzal, wings and back a heavenly green
the turquoise-blue of the spangled cotinga, its throat, plum-red

the Japanese blue-and-white flycatcher
the quietness of its beauty doubles the gift

Light

a riverside dawn of roseate spoonbills
an azure kingfisher's first dive, riddling the new sky

a sunburst of yellow-rumped thornbills
a zenith of orange-breasted buntings

a jazz, a jizz, of blue-eared glossy starlings
a candle tree of emerald starlings

a sunset lagoon of flamingos
a gloaming of *porphyrio porphyrio*

Icons

eagles, used to configure the hauteur, the cruelty, of absolute power –
on crests, pendants, seal rings, their wings flapping on flags

the power of beauty, looking back at the beholder:
habitué of paradise gardens, of poetry; under the thumb on Indian coins

armoured with emeralds, Jamaica's red-billed streamertail hovers
on stamps, banknotes; in sanctuaries will perch on a fingertip to sip syrup

kiwi, living so quietly close to the earth, the only bird
with marrow in its bones; guarded by Tāne Mahuta, god of the forest

Sacred Space

a basilica of swallows
a sanctuary-lamp flicker of phoenixes

a holy ghostliness of doves
a muralled dome with aerial choir – their haloes, oriole-yellow

on a chapel wall, *Madonna and Child with Goldfinch*
a mosaic of Francis with wrens, larks, siskins

an iconostasis of swan wings, angel wings
on a clerestory ledge, a nest of sparrows

Church

a stained-glass window, cracked,
with kingfisher, cross-winged cormorant

a gargoyle spout, the haunt of jackdaws
a carved lectern's eagle, wings spread for flight

a collage of red cardinals
in filigreed bowers, the black-winged red bishops

a vulning of pelicans
a de profundis of bitterns

The Body Politic

an ascendancy of pied currawongs
a gentry of capercallies

a clergy of cassowaries
an elect of letter-winged kites

a boardroom of vampire finches
a mortgage bank of brush cuckoos

a parliament of shufflewings
a public monument of pigeons

In Twilight

the Bird Room: a limbo of restive wings,
eyes keyed with ambivalent light

on the walls, painted tableaux of birds
posed in airless Edens

a Cabinet of Curiosity with flamingo skull,
rafter-hung heron,

drawer after drawer of blown eggs,
minutely flecked

Museum

in jewelled shrouds
a tiny universe of hummingbirds

whose wings once sang,
on their best for two centuries

birds of the woodlands, bright of feather or discreet,
each holding its secret, still

horned owls in a perpetual dusk
watching from behind crystal eyes

Extinction

a hypothesis of dodo bird
a shooting spree, century-long, of passenger pigeons

the elephant bird, the ivory-billed woodpecker
the Hawai'i mamo, its beak down-curved to tap lobelia nectar

the Aldabra rail, absent for twenty millennia, now back –
the only bird to become flightless, twice

a library of stories, untold, unread, unknown,
hidden beneath tree roots, glacier and grass plain, windy uplands

Threnody

a necropolis of sacred ibis
bone middens of the great auk

a diorama of laughing owls
a netsuke-cull of helmeted hornbills

a tray of hummingbirds, cold, sold for love charms
a ghost forest, felled long ago, aglimmer with Carolina parakeets

a fossil record of *Ichthyornis*
a living memory of huias

The Poetry of Birds

Mary Oliver's white owl leaving, five feet apart on snow,
'the imprint of the tips of its wings'

'beating up from Senegal', the ospreys of Kathleen Jamie – bound for
a Scots pine, their nest 'gale-battered, winter-worn, half toppled away'

Moya Cannon's one-legged flycatcher, 'balancing her tiny, tattered body',
migrates south – returns 'to raise brood after brood' in a Philadelphia hedge

Dickinson's hummingbird, each wing 'a revolving Wheel',
its body 'a Resonance of Emerald – a Rush of Cochineal'

The Art of Birds

a Brancusi of bird-in-flight
an echelon of shelducks on a wall

an Audubon of Carolina parakeets
an Elizabeth Gould of helmeted honeyeaters

a John Wolseley of spiny-cheeked honeyeaters
a Jim Dine of ravens, outlined in gold

a Matisse of white doves
a Picasso of white doves

Voices

an introit of blackbirds
a tuning fork of cuckoos

a descant of dunnocks
an undersong of rooks

an uproar of kookaburras
a fanfare of trumpeter swans

a canticle of bobolinks
a consolation of mopokes

Music

a Vivaldi of goldfinches
a violin crescendo of lark

a Handel songbook of silver dove, turtle dove, phoenix
a Pastoral Symphony of quail, cuckoo, nightingale

a Papageno of chaffinches, warblers
hens, courtesy of Rameau, Respighi, Saint-Saëns

a forest of bird calls transcribed by Messiaen
a sound-wreath by William Barton of birdsong at dusk

Coda

Monterey Cypress, White Cockatoos

Most, grey-toned under the gaunt green eaves,
the outliers, ablaze… They could be auditioning for

letters in a new alphabet, or testing out
reverse points of view, provocative takes –

all the while feasting with friends. Why even notice
that figure below, part of nature's wallpaper,

a patch of white in hand, listening to a sound
as of light, sharp rain falling. The bay gleams on.

The Moments

To the Wildlife Photographers

1. In the Realm of the Penguins

Iceberg, 1995

'Blue Ice and Penguins' – Cherry Alexander

Ancient ice, a fusion of bedrock blue
and white at its most elusive –

those upward sweeps crowned by
cloud-like scribbles, curlicues of scrim.

A prion flies darkly, heroically past
chinstrap penguins, compact as a Greek chorus,

resting on one incarnation of water above another.
Timelessly, the waves heave by.

Surfacing

'Bubble-Jetting Emperors' – Paul Nicklen

The smooth bowls of their bellies –
perfect for tobogganing. Feet than can march for hours…

And now, those sea-wings come into their own
as hundreds, somewhat heavier than in descent,

bubble-jet from the depths, leaving
oblique, pale-blue trails as they make for

a roughed-up surface, that edge of ice,
the sunlight coming to meet them.

Bouncing Back

'Frozen Moment' – Paul Nicklen

This, the only time they can be said to fly –
and it is spectacular:

emperor penguins exiting the ocean
sky-rocket as high as two metres

back onto the ice – where leopard seals
may be waiting to welcome them.

Dive upwards, leap as far and fast as you can,
toboggan the snowy miles back to your chicks.

The Moment

'If Penguins Could Fly' – Eduardo del Álamo

The photographer expects this moment –
but not the gentoo penguin

(fastest swimmer of all the penguins)
at rest on a fragment of ice.

The leopard seal swimming back and forth
now rises as if from an unseen cavern –

so huge, so swift, that mouth so wide.
The odds on escape so very long.

The Line

'Snow Kings' – Ole Jørgen Liodden

Sporadic assaults of whiteness –
veil upon veil of oblivion.

Regardless, these penguins place
one miraculous foot in front of the other

and press unrelentingly forward,
looking at brine, sleet or clearing air –

each sleekly stalwart body behind another
as they head home to feed their young.

On Marion Island

'The Plumage Parade' – Thomas P. Peschak

Macaroni penguins in single-file
wind through a lava-ravaged, green landscape

to reach their roosting terraces
high on this volcano peak.

Within hours a storm will take hold
driving most of them to march back down

to the bracing upheavals, the perils
known and unknown, of the kingdom of krill.

Sun-up

'Three Kings' – Wim Van Den Heever

Shore waves wash new light into the sea
wherein, soon, their unreadable eyes

will seek out lantern fish and squid –
these three, now living out another drama:

the two males fending each other off, vying for
the female who stands so still, so grounded,

her orange-trimmed beak pointed skywards:
auburn clouds, dazzle of yellow, ice-white sun.

Partnership

'Training Session' – Stefan-Christmann

The bills of emperor penguins, so we learn,
reflect UV light: a feature males may employ

to attract a mate, along with ecstatic displays –
their calling card – at places of promise in the throng.

When the choice is made, the pair will align,
perform mirror dances, learn each other's calls.

They'll raise one chick, companion each other
beneath skies glacial or auroral.

Ritual

'The Art of Conception' – Stefan Christmann

Before mating, emperor penguins
bow low to each other.

Their act of union –
unstable, necessarily brief –

is, yet, a balance of
graceful, dynamic lines:

his head bent over, hers curved back
in the moment of creation.

The Five Thousand

'The Huddle' – Stefan Christmann

Look closer. Across this sea of indigo-grey,
this mass of pouched, brooding males,

a few heads are raised – breathing clearly,
their unseeable eyes reading the wider view.

In that slowly transforming huddle,
all take turns on the windward side.

Each one, magnificently, waits without waiting,
works at continuance, guards a new life.

Eye

'Cradle of Life' – Stefan Christmann

A new eye, looking out
before the stained shell is fully broken,

the chick not yet known to itself,
its form, egg-shaped but complete,

soon, soon, to become a presence in the world,
learning a slow thriving

until ready to mate and to nurture,
to forage deep below the sun's swaying eye.

Tending

'Bond of Life' – Stefan Christmann

That beak poised above the chick
will caress, preen nascent feathers,

deliver, from its crop, sustenance,
and issue calls that answer the chick's own –

a connecting thread, antiphonal –
so that, when it begins to wander

or a parent returns, well-stocked, from the sea,
the chick is found inside the colony, tended.

Huddling Chicks

'Fluff Formation' – Stefan Christmann

Most keep their heads down,
pale grey backs, dark necks, crusted with ice.

For those at the warm centre,
the luxury of looking up.

But they, too, will learn to survive
communally, dwell for a time on the edge

where the blizzard hits hardest.
One for all, and all for one.

Small Crèche

'A Mother's Courage' – Linc Gasking

The body language of fear –
the nearly grown chicks clumped together, screaming.

The body language of bravery – beak open, flippers held wide,
the minder, ready to fight back, sacrifice herself.

The predator – a carrion eater, drowner of gannets, albatrosses –
simply stands and looks, deciding.

The drama is set forth as on a stage: desist or destroy?
surrender or stand firm? The sounds of terror, of defiance.

Group Portrait

'Teamwork' – Stefan Christmann

The first penguins stood, it is said, two metres high.
Over aeons, their wisdom brought them to this

compact bulk, this streamlined strength, endowed them
with the power to endure, until now, all weathers.

Here they are, each in their own true space –
a community of knowledge and feeling.

Whenever one comes, calling for its mate,
the voices of those nearby fall silent.

Ice

'Meeting Place' – Yaz Loukhal

Stillness they know, more than any other creature,
every moment the right moment.

On Snow Hill island, in a village without shelter
they are grouped – dense nucleus

with a scatter of outliers; the rhythm
of generations marking the whole design.

Amid so much white space, white noise,
this indwelling together.

The Wildlife Photographers

'… the cold felt like needles piercing my fingertips.'
– Stefan Christmann, on photographing 'The Huddle'

When the moment comes, the gloves must come off,
even at forty below, to focus the lens on this two-month huddle.

Or, there's a rough sea journey, a helicopter flight,
the long trudge through thick snow to witness, from afar,

with wonder, a lone colony of emperor penguins.
Or, with legs locked under a lip of ice, the submerged wait

for penguins speeding from the depths. Or, that blizzard crouch
to conjure a homebound procession, white within white.

Dive

'The Final Leap' – Stefan Christmann

This emperor penguin's the first to dive
from the ice shelf into its image

on level water. The others wait.
There's been a two-week trek, shadowed by

a photographer in quest of this moment –
the moment of return to ocean's sustenance.

Eight eight-metre dives. In the distance
ice floes like clouds on the sea's sky-grey.

Aurora Australis

'Disco Lights Antarctic Style' – Stefan Christmann

A violet sky hung with folds
of incandescent green.

Emperor penguins are returning home to each other
and to their chicks, corralled in a crèche.

This festival of colour cleaves the six-month darkness –
a time of bleak endurance, of resurgence:

loss and growth lived out
beneath a dusting of stars.

The Long Moment

'Taking in the Vista' – Stefan Christmann

September. These emperor penguins
have translated themselves, early,

from a colony on sea ice where they paired up,
raised their chicks, to this ice shelf.

Above a white ocean, the azure of its horizon
tuned to that deeper blue within the ice,

they enhance the stillness,
stand amidst a panorama of new light.

2. Sightings

Chilean Flamingos

Junji Takasago at Salar de Uyuni, Bolivia

A frieze of flamingos
on the world's largest salt flat:

beauty, at high altitude
taking, in fact, your breath away.

Each preening bird, dusky pink, stands above
an inverted self in cloud water.

All else, a covenant between
white and cerulean. The stillness, numinous.

Lesser Flamingos

Paul Souders at Lake Natron, Tanzania

Ol Doinyo Lengai mountain
casts an image, equally deep blue,

onto Natron's shallow waters:
below its cratered summit

thousands upon thousands of
pink flamingos nesting –

reefs and wreaths of them
arrayed on cloud shine.

Tropicbirds

Tropicbirds photographed by Peter Norvig

A trio of tropicbirds flying fast, high,
above a sea of blue shadows.

At this moment, the tail streamers of one
drape over the wing of another

casting two tendril-fine shadows onto it,
while that bird's own streamers

seem to rest along a wing of the third.
So fast, so high, yet staying in touch.

Flying Puffin

'Late Delivery' – Catherine Dobbins D'Alessio

Puffins may seem, to my captive eyes,
too ingeniously exquisite

to dig burrows, hunt deep in the changing sea.
But here, beak crammed with krill,

one flies through evening light
in a no-nonsense way

back to its cliffside home where,
frail in the darkness, a puffling whistles its need.

Grebes: the Token

'Sunrise Performance' – Mateusz Piesiak

The fact of an irradiated sprig
hanging above them like mistletoe,

and the way their bodies are now outlined
by that same amber gold –

burnishing, too, their liquid shadows –
means nothing to them.

But a gift of waterweed, with its twirly
flourish of dawn light, begins the courtship.

Grebe with Grebettes

'Eat Up Your Feathers' – David Pattyn

She's programmed to do this:
pluck feathers from her breast

and feed them to the stripy triad
cached between her wings.

Greater intestinal fortitude will result –
the sheathing of bones from the fish

they'll soon ingest and, in time, swipe
from weedy, shadowy, slow-moving deeps.

This Particular Rock

'Dipper Dispute' – Heikki Nikke

With the ceremonial parity
of a courtship dance, this aerial contest:

at issue, a 'dipping' rock –
vantage point and launch pad.

Drops, flung from four wings, star the air;
water threads twist below two claws.

Up in the sunlight, eyeball to eyeball.
The stream a churning conduit of riches.

Turquoise Kingfisher, Diving

'The Blue Trail' – Mario Cea

If it flies fast enough, in the right light,
this bird's image will show a wake in air –

a streak of luminous blue glimpsed against
the pond's darker waters – a trail not present

beneath its reflection on bright water.
For the kingfisher: one of countless daily dives.

For the photographer: six months,
two thousand tries, to get this improbable shot.

Pit Stop, Poland

'Dunlin Panorama' – Mateusz Piesiak

A passing falcon has triggered
this hurried, flurried leaving –

dunlins rise against the clouds
but for minutes only: then back, down

to this unruly shoreline, its reed beds
strewn with jewel hoards of crustaceans,

a myriad insects for the taking.
Southern Europe, northwest Africa, can wait.

Unharvested Field

'Brambling Bonanza' – Mateusz Piesiak

Yes, this is paradise.
Boulevards of lanterns

full of, not light,
but the stuff of life.

And, surrounded by husks,
stuff them down you do – sunflower seeds,

each one fuel for minutes of flight,
an increment of the onward journey.

Dead of Winter

'Cool Drink' – Diana Rebman

In this nadir of cold
a company of long-tailed tits

visit an icicle in turns,
a kind of dance –

flying and hovering so fast,
nibbling away for dear life.

At moments, a winged icicle,
white, amid so much whiteness.

Eurasian Bullfinch

'Eurasian Bullfinch' – Wojtek Rygielski

Were this finch a landscape, it would be
a field of sunlit blooms cut by shadow.

Sublimely in contrast with itself,
fusing the two solstices, this bird has solved

a conundrum without becoming one.
Perched on a scaly winter branch, it sports

a peachy portliness that would suggest,
if not for its wings, an unflappable assurance.

Lesser Blue-eared Starling

'Eye-light' – Nicola de Sario

Before the sun has fully set
a starling is pictured in black-and-white,

the blue-green iridescence of its plumage
done with for the day

along with all the here-and-there flights
and a small part in an epic of murmuration.

But its eye is a power in this near darkness:
a full moon with a new moon inside it.

The Courtship of Ravens

'The Intimate Touch' – Shane Kalyn

After the flying wing-to-wing, the dancing,
the mutual preening, this is a perfect seal of trust:

the touching of beaks, the entering of them;
that icy half-drop of water catching the light.

Winter has stalled the world. But these are ravens,
possessed of so much knowledge, so much care.

Gifts of moss and twigs; soothing comfort sounds.
The faceted glaze of black feathers, set against snow.

Great Grey Owls: a Family Portrait

'Dinner Duty' – Tommy Pedersen

'Snow-plungers'. Their flight as silent as snow.
At rest, a cryptic grandeur.

The mother's wing enfolds their last nestling;
the father holds the kill, the key.

They are one entity,
a construct of power and vulnerability.

Home is a tree hollow, the forest a living trove,
night, dawn and dusk are their domain.

Ural Owls, Red Squirrel

'Surprise!' – Makoto Ando

An owl couple – so still.
Why ruffle one's composure for

a squirrel – a family meal, true –
squirrelling itself away?

In this woodland woven with tiny
enticing sounds, there is always later.

The ways of owls are so slow
except when they're not.

So it is

'Night Hunter' – Jonas Classon

An overlay of midnight blue
unifying everything

except that pearl-white full moon
poised above the head of

a great grey owl, one claw raised,
its eyes a smoulder of intention.

Outside the frame, deep in a field,
the last seconds of a vole.

Long-eared Owl

'Last Light' – Mateusz Piesiak

Beauty and death, packaged.
Even so, that smallness is endearing.

I look at the space around this owl,
the intimate context of branches, and think:

that would be a good image to die with –
framed by an uplift of strength, such airy prospects.

Even in near sleep, those wizard eyes and ears
delve, touch the tremulous.

Song

'The Smallest Songster' – Nooa Mikkola

So small as to bypass attention, almost –
there, on a Norway spruce, in low light.

In conifer forests of Europe, of Asia,
it abounds – a plain bird

but with gold where it counts.
Now – as I write this, or as you read this –

countless goldcrests are offering a song,
a royal gift, to the world.

Grey-breasted Wood Wren

'The Listening Bird' – Nick Kanakis

I thought, at first, you must be
dead – down there among the leaf litter:

its dark browns matching yours,
shades of tan and ochre streaked with damp.

Your body lies sideways, claw touching throat,
the sky a swatch of brightness in your eye.

Your own voice, melodious or rasping, on hold,
you geolocate other kinds of music.

Notes

Notes

The Mirrors

Quotations and factual material were drawn from the following sources:

Flamingo, Caitlin R. Kight (Reaktion Books, 2015)

Flamingo Hunt, Paul A. Zahl (Bobbs Merrill, 1952)

The San Diego Zoo. See: San Diego Zoo. https://animals.sandiegozoo.org/animals/flamingo

Data regarding the flamingos Greater and Chile can be found on the websites of Adelaide Zoo and the South Australian Museum. In the latter, a display case containing the taxidermied remains of the two flamingos was installed in November, 2021. See: adelaidezoo.com.au; samuseum.sa.gov.au

p.17 See: wikimedia commons, 'Flamingos at the Adelaide Zoo' (GN04379).jpg

p.21 See: 'Prehistoric pink flamingos once walked the arid zones of Central Australia' by Emma Haskin, *The New Daily*, 14 March 2018.

p.23 The quote is from a passage in John J. Audubon's *The Birds of America, volume 6,* regarding Plate 431, 'American Flamingo':

> When I reached Key West, my first inquiries, addressed to Dr. Benjamin Strobel, had reference to the Flamingoes, and I felt gratified by learning that he had killed a good number of them, and that he would assist us in procuring some. As on that Key they are fond of resorting to the shallow ponds formerly kept there as reservoirs of water, for the purpose of making salt, we visited them at different times, but always without success; and, although I saw a great number of them in the course of my stay in that country, I cannot even at this moment boast of having had the satisfaction of shooting a single individual.

John Tenniel illustrated the first edition of *Alice in Wonderland* (1865).

p.25 Mark D. Anderson. See: http://www.savetheflamingo.co.za

p.28 Section 3: see entry for p.66, given on pp.103-4 of Notes.

Zoo Birds
p.43 The orange-bellied parrot is a critically endangered Victorian bird.

Company Terms
pp.51-2 In l.3, 'a quell of kingfishers' alludes to a Greek myth wherein Alcyone and Ceyx were harshly punished by Zeus. In recompense, the gods changed them into kingfishers and becalmed the sea winds for two weeks during the nesting period of the kingfisher – 'halcyon' in Greek. Thus the phrase, 'halcyon days'.

l.8 alludes to an image of woods lit by owl eyes in the film *Reaching for the Moon* (2013).

l.42. 'What is the price of two sparrows – one copper coin? But not a single sparrow can fall to the ground without your Father knowing it.' – *Matthew 10:29*.

l.47. The critically endangered white-bellied cinclodes, a member of the ovenbird family, is found only at extremely high elevations in the Andes of central Peru.

l.48. The kākāpō, a New Zealand ground parrot, is critically threatened.

l.50. '91%. The estimated decline in the nightingale population in Britain between 1967 and 2007.' – *Independent*, 21 June 2010.

'A nightingale's tiny larynx can reputedly produce four notes at once, even with its mouth full.' – Simon Jenkins, 'Must we silence nightingales in order to build houses?', *Guardian*, 19 April 2013.

A Summoning of Birds
p.58 In 'Presences', 'a playfulness of loons' alludes to a passage in Chapter 12 of Henry David Thoreau's *Walden*:

> It was a pretty game, played on the smooth surface of the pond, a man against a loon. Suddenly your adversary's checker disappears beneath the board, and the problem is to place yours nearest to where his will appear again. Sometimes he would come up unexpectedly on the opposite side of me, having apparently passed directly under the boat…

p.59 'In Motion', l.3. 'As the ornithologist Edward Howe Forbush once observed, "I have seen a chickadee drop over backward from a branch in pursuit of an insect, catch it, and turning an almost complete somersault in the air, strike right side up again on the leaning trunk of the tree."' – Jennifer Ackerman, *The Genius of Birds*.
l.4 refers to a video clip, viewed on YouTube, of a tame white cockatoo, Snowball, dancing to a soundtrack of breakdance music.

p.61 'Stratagems', l.1. Cormorants have been used by humans for centuries to dive, catch and deliver fish. Little black cormorants often hunt in co-ordinated groups, herding small fish so as to catch them from the surface.
l.2. Older offspring may assist in raising new broods of fairy wrens.
l.3. The New Caledonian crow's use of tools is unmatched in the bird world.
l.4. '… a single [Clark's] nutcracker will gather more than thirty thousand pine seeds in a single summer, carrying up to one hundred seeds at a time in a special large pouch under its tongue. These it buries in up to five thousand different caches scattered throughout a territory of dozens, even hundreds, of square miles. Then it later finds the scattered treasures.' – Jennifer Ackerman, *The Genius of Birds*.

p.62 'Nests', l.2. 'quarrion', another word for 'cockatiel', derives from 'guwarrayiŋ' in the Wiradhuri language.

p.64 'Threat'. ll.3-4 allude to a scene in the film *Winged Migration* (2001).

p.65 'Murmurations', l.2. Wolfgang Amadeus Mozart kept a pet starling for three years until its death. At their first meeting, the starling copied the (sung or whistled?) opening bars of the third movement of his *Piano Concerto No. 17*.
'Glimpse'. ll.3-4 refer to a photograph, titled 'Curved line of pelicans in the sky near island mountain', credited to JPaulB on: istockphoto.com
l.8. The plumage of the trumpet manucode is a glossy blue-black. The word 'manucode' derives from the Malay *manuq dewata*, 'bird of the gods'.

p.66 'Apparitions', l.2. 'Magpies recognise their own image in a mirror… When experimenters placed a red dot on the throat of six magpies, two of them tried to scratch off the dot on their own bodies with their legs, rather than reacting to the image in the mirror.' – Jennifer Ackerman, *The Genius of Birds*.

ll.3-4. See: 'Image of herons nesting high in the treetops wins drone photo award', by Gege Li, in *New Scientist*, 11 Nov 2020.

p.68 'A Litany of Colour'. John Gould named the Gouldian finch in honour of his wife, Elizabeth, after her death. Her major contribution of artistic work for *The Birds of Australia*, written by John Gould, went largely unrecognised. See: https://australiapostcollectables.com.au/articles/elizabeth-gould-and-the-birds-of-australia

p.71 'Church', l.2. In Christian iconography, a kingfisher can symbolise resurrection, a cormorant with outstretched wings may evoke Christ on the cross.

l.5. Red cardinal birds, (only the male is red), are named after cardinals in the Catholic church, with their bright red garments and hats that might suggest the crest atop the bird. One collective noun for a group of clerical cardinals is 'college'.

l.7. The belief that pelicans wounded their breasts to feed blood to their starving young led to its use as a Christ-image. 'vulnus' is the Latin word for 'wound'.

'The Body Politic', l.4. The letter-winged kite has a black line like the letter 'W' (or 'M') on the undersides of its wings.

p.72 'In Twilight', ll.1-4. On Karl Russ's legendary bird room, see Bernd Brunner's *Birdmania: A Remarkable Passion for Birds* (Allen & Unwin, 2017).

p.73 'Extinction', ll.5-6. See: 'Extinct Bird Re-Evolved Itself Back Into Existence', by Alexa Lardieri, in *U.S. News & World Report*, 10 May 2019. 'Threnody', l.4. The helmeted hornbill is critically endangered because of the use of its casque by ivory carvers for netsukes and other items.

p.74 'The Poetry of Birds'. Mary Oliver, 'White Owl Flies Into and Out of the Field', *House of Light*. Kathleen Jamie, 'Ospreys', *The Overhaul*. Moya Cannon, 'Fly-Catcher', *Keats Lives*. Emily Dickinson, 'A Route of

Evanescence', poem 1463 in *The Complete Poems of Emily Dickinson*, ed. Thomas H. Johnson.

'The Art of Birds', l.3. See John J. Audubon's *The Birds of America*, Plate 26. l.4. Elizabeth Gould's lithograph, 'Helmeted Honeyeaters', is in *Birds of Australia*. This Victorian bird is critically endangered.

p.75 'Music'. l.2 alludes to Vaughan Williams' *The Lark Ascending*. l.5. Papageno, a bird-catcher, appears in Mozart's *The Magic Flute*. l.8. William Barton's *Birdsong at Dusk* features on the CD of that name (ABC Classics, 2014).

The Moments

Many of the photographs written about in 'The Moments' can be found on the website of the Natural History Museum in London, England, having featured in its annual *Wildlife Photographer of the Year* competition. Most of these can be accessed via photographer's name and photograph title. Links are provided for other photographs where possible. Some photographers have their own websites.

p.79 'Iceberg, 1995' *'Blue Ice and Penguins' – Cherry Alexander*
https://www.nhm.ac.uk/discover/women-in-wildlife-photography.html
'Surfacing' *'Bubble-Jetting Emperors' – Paul Nicklen*
https://www.nhm.ac.uk/wpy/gallery/2012-bubble-jetting-emperors

p.80 'Bouncing Back' *'Frozen Moment' – Paul Nicklen*
https://www.nhm.ac.uk/wpy/gallery/2012-frozen-moment
'The Moment' *'If Penguins Could Fly' – Eduardo del Álamo*
https://www.nhm.ac.uk/wpy/gallery/2019-if-penguins-could-fly

p.81 'The Line' *'Snow Kings' – Ole Jørgen Liodden*
https://www.nhm.ac.uk/wpy/gallery/2011-snow-kings
'On Marion Island' '*The Plumage Parade' – Thomas P. Peschak*
https://www.nhm.ac.uk/wpy/gallery/2019-the-plumage-parade

p.82 'Sun-up' *'Three Kings'* – *Wim Van Den Heever*
https://www.nhm.ac.uk/wpy/gallery/2018-three-kings
'Partnership' *'Training Session'* – *Stefan Christmann*
https://nature-in-focus.de/stills_emperors/ Still No. 14

p.83 'Ritual' *'The Art of Conception'* – *Stefan Christmann*
https://www.nhm.ac.uk/wpy/gallery/2019-the-art-of-conception
'The Five Thousand' *'The Huddle'* – *Stefan Christmann*
https://www.nhm.ac.uk/wpy/gallery/2019-the-huddle

p.84 'Eye' *'Cradle of Life'* – *Stefan Christmann*
https://www.nhm.ac.uk/wpy/gallery/2019-cradle-of-life
'Tending' *'Bond of Life'* – *Stefan Christmann*
https://www.nhm.ac.uk/wpy/gallery/2019-bond-of-life

p.85 'Huddling Chicks' *'Fluff Formation'* – *Stefan Christmann*
https://www.nhm.ac.uk/wpy/gallery/2019-fluff-formation
'Small Crèche' *'A Mother's Courage'* – *Linc Gasking*
https://www.nhm.ac.uk/wpy/gallery/2015-a-mothers-courage

p.86 'Group Portrait' *'Teamwork'* – *Stefan Christmann*
https://nature-in-focus.de/stills_emperors/ Still No. 30
'Ice' *'Meeting Place'* – *Yaz Loukhal* https://yazloukhal.com/awards

p.87 'The Wildlife Photographers' See details given above for:
'The Huddle' – *Stefan Christmann*, ('The Five Thousand'); *'Meeting Place'* –
Yaz Loukhal, ('Ice'); *'Bubble-Jetting Emperors'* – *Paul Nicklen*, ('Surfacing');
'Snow Kings' – *Ole Jørgen Liodden*, ('The Line').
'Dive' *'The Final Leap'* – *Stefan Christmann*
https://www.nhm.ac.uk/wpy/gallery/2019-the-final-leap

p.88 'Aurora Australis' *'Disco Lights Antarctic Style'* – *Stefan Christmann*
https://nature-in-focus.de/stills_emperors/ Still No. 7
'The Long Moment' *'Taking in the Vista'* – *Stefan Christmann*
https://nature-in-focus.de/stills_emperors/ Still No. 11

Stefan Christmann has provided this comment on *Taking in the Vista*:

> 'The birds on the ice shelf were photographed roughly in September when snow ramps have formed between the sea ice and the ice shelf which allow the birds to climb up onto the year round stable ice shelf. It is believed to be one adaptation strategy that "buys time" for the penguins in case there is an early break up of the sea ice.'

p.89 'Chilean Flamingos' *'Heavenly Flamingos' – Junji Takasago*
https://www.nhm.ac.uk/wpy/gallery/2022-heavenly-flamingos
'Lesser Flamingos' Paul Souders' photograph, 'Africa, Tanzania, Aerial view of Ol Doinyo Lengai volcano looming above vast flock of Lesser Flamingos nesting in shallow salt waters of Lake Natron', features on various websites.

p.90 'Tropicbirds' Peter Norvig's photograph can be found at:
https://pn.smugmug.com/keyword/tropic%20bird/i-BTLb4p2/A
'Flying Puffin' *'Late Delivery' – Catherine Dobbins D'Alessio*
https://www.nhm.ac.uk/wpy/gallery/2020-late-delivery

p.91 'Grebes: the Token' *'Sunrise Performance' – Mateusz Piesiak*
https://www.nhm.ac.uk/wpy/gallery/2022-sunrise-performance
'Grebe with Grebettes' *'Eat Up Your Feathers' – David Pattyn*
https://www.nhm.ac.uk/wpy/gallery/2022-eat-up-your-feathers

p.92 'This Particular Rock' *'Dipper Dispute' – Heikki Nikke*
https://www.nhm.ac.uk/wpy/gallery/2022-dipper-dispute
'Turquoise Kingfisher, Diving' *'The Blue Trail' – Mario Cea*
https://www.nhm.ac.uk/wpy/gallery/2016-the-blue-trail
https://mymodernmet.com/mario-cea-kingfisher-bird-photo/

p.93 'Pit Stop, Poland' *'Dunlin Panorama' – Mateusz Piesiak*
https://www.nhm.ac.uk/wpy/gallery/2022-dunlin-panorama
'Unharvested Field' *'Brambling Bonanza' – Mateusz Piesiak*
https://www.nhm.ac.uk/wpy/gallery/2022-brambling-bonanza

p.94 'Dead of Winter' *'Cool Drink' – Diana Rebman*
https://www.nhm.ac.uk/wpy/gallery/2019-cool-drink
'Eurasian Bullfinch' *'Eurasian Bullfinch' – Wojtek Rygielski*
https://rygielski.net/791/

p.95 'Lesser Blue-eared Starling' *'Eye-light' – Nicola de Sario*
https://www.nhm.ac.uk/wpy/gallery/2016-eyelight
'The Courtship of Ravens' *'The Intimate Touch' – Shane Kalyn*
https://www.nhm.ac.uk/wpy/gallery/2021-the-intimate-touch

p.96 'Great Grey Owls: a Family Portrait' *'Dinner Duty' – Tommy Pedersen*
https://www.nhm.ac.uk/wpy/gallery/2019-dinner-duty
'Ural Owls, Red Squirrel' *'Surprise!' – Makoto Ando*
https://www.nhm.ac.uk/wpy/gallery/2020-surprise

p.97 'So it is' *'Night Hunter' – Jonas Classon*
https://www.nhm.ac.uk/wpy/gallery/2020-night-hunter
'Long-eared Owl' *'Last Light' – Mateusz Piesiak*
https://www.nhm.ac.uk/wpy/gallery/2013-last-light

p.98 'Song' *'The Smallest Songster' – Nooa Mikkola*
https://www.nhm.ac.uk/wpy/gallery/2022-the-smallest-songster
'Grey-breasted Wood Wren' *'The Listening Bird' – Nick Kanakis*
https://www.nhm.ac.uk/wpy/gallery/2022-the-listening-bird

Acknowledgements

I acknowledge the support of the Victorian Government through Creative Victoria for a literary grant to support the writing of 'Zoo Birds' and other poems.

*

Poems have appeared in the online journals *Axon, Cordite Poetry Review, Live Encounters Poetry and Writing*, and in the anthologies, *Best Australian Poems, 2017* (Black Inc., Melbourne, 2017) and *Signs: the University of Canberra Vice-Chancellor's International Poetry Prize, 2018.*

'Bird of prey centre', in 'Zoo Birds', appeared initially in Diane Fahey's poetry collection, *The Stone Garden: Poems from Clare* (Clouds of Magellan, 2013).

*

In addition to the observation of birds in many natural settings, *Sanctuaries* includes poems written in response to visits to the following: Healesville Sanctuary, the Zoological Gardens of Melbourne and of Adelaide, Taronga Zoo in Sydney and Jurong Bird Park, Singapore.

*

My warm thanks to Stefan Christmann for his permission to reproduce *Taking in the Vista* on the cover, where it appears in an edited form, and for providing information about some of his photographs.

*

I live and write on Wadawurrung Country, and acknowledge the Traditional Custodians, past, present and future, of this place.

Milton Keynes UK
Ingram Content Group UK Ltd.
UKHW040627190824
447134UK00001B/76